RELATIVELY ROYAL

A personal view

Robert Golden

With affectionate memories of

DOROTHY

The Marchioness of Cambridge,
who provided much laughter and encouragement

Published by

ROSVALL
ROYAL BOOKS
Enasen – Falekvarna
521 91 FALKÖPING, Sweden
tel: 46-515-37105 fax: 46-515-37165
e-mail: ted.rosvall@telia.com

ISBN 91-973978-1-4
Elanders Gummessons, Falköping 2000

FRONT COVER
The Marchioness of Cambridge photographed in her Coronation Robes at Kensington Palace in 1953. She is wearing a large diamond sunburst brooch, which had belonged to the first Duchess of Westminster. Her pearls had belonged to Queen Charlotte and the tiara to the first Duchess of Cambridge. The lace at her sleeves was taken from her wedding dress of 1923, and she is also wearing the Silver Jubilee Medal of 1935 and the 1937 Coronation Medal. Her robes as a Marchioness are now kept at Kensington Palace as part of the Court Costume Collection.

BACK COVER
The wedding of Prince George of Battenberg and Countess Nada Torby which took place in 1916. There were two services. The first one being held at the then Russian Church in Buckingham Palace Road followed by an Anglican service at the Chapel Royal, St James's Palace. The bridal party then drove to Kenwood House, the home of her parents, for the wedding reception where this photograph was taken. Left to right: the bridegroom, his sister, Princess Louise of Battenberg, the bride, wearing traditional Russian head dress, her sister, Countess Zia Torby and two cousins, Princesses Xenia and Nina of Russia. This was the fifth occasion that a descendant of Queen Victoria had married into the Romanov Dynasty. Her second son, Alfred, Duke of Edinburgh, married in 1874 Grand Duchess Marie, daughter of Emperor Alexander II, whilst his daughter, Princess Victoria Melita, married as her second husband, Grand Duke Kirill in 1905. Two daughters of Princess Alice, Grand Duchess of Hesse, also joined the ranks of the Russian Imperial Family; Princess Elisabeth becoming Grand Duchess Serge in 1884 and her sister, Alexandra, marrying Tsar Nicholas II in 1894.

ACKNOWLEDGMENTS

I wish to thank H.M. The Queen for gracious permission to use material from the Royal Photographic Archives and the following for their assistance in providing material and support: The late Lady May Abel Smith, Argyll Etkin Ltd., the late Mary, Duchess of Beaufort, Mr Harold Brown, the late Marchioness of Cambridge, Mrs Anne Grainger, Mr Liam Kennedy, the Hon Mrs Gerald Lascelles, Mrs Karen Liddell-Grainger, Janet, Marchioness of Milford Haven, the late Lady Tatiana Mountbatten, Mr Peter Murray, Mr Robin Piguet, Mr Peter Russell, Mrs Marjorie Smeeth, Mr David Stanley, The Hugo Vickers Collection, the late Lady Mary Whitley, Mr David Williamson and Mr Trevor Wilson. A special thanks to Robert Horley for helping with the typescript and the pedigrees; Ms Pamela Peltonen, who completed the typescript at a marathon sitting in Helsinki, my sister, Mrs Linda Maloney, who painstakingly did the proof reading, making several constructive suggestions and my publisher, Mr Ted Rosvall, for providing an eye-catching title and for having faith in this project.

This does not pretend to be a complete record of all the minor members of the Royal Family. Some, such as Earl and Countess Mountbatten, enjoyed a high profile lifestyle making them public figures in their own right. Others, who include Lord Leopold Mountbatten and the 2nd Duke of Connaught, died young, while the Earl of Harewood and his brother, the Hon Gerald Lascelles, led full-time professional lives. Therefore, few photographs are included of them as individuals, though they are represented as part of larger groups.

November 2000

Robert Golden
The Lodge – Gore Rd
London E9 7HR
England

Robert Golden, who lives in London, regularly contributes royal obituaries to The Daily Telegraph, has written articles for Royalty Digest and, as a spokesman for Debrett's Peerage, has spoken on the wireless and appeared on BBC News 24. Recently, he took part in a BBC tribute to Queen Elizabeth The Queen Mother. He was a close friend of the Marchioness of Cambridge and Lady May Abel Smith and their families, who provided him with many of the photographs in this book. Lady Cambridge had long urged him to produce a book of this sort and she and Lady May Abel Smith were the sources for many of the anecdotes. Through Lady Cambridge he met other members of the Royal Family. He accompanied her and the Duke of Beaufort from St James' Palace to St Paul's Cathedral for the wedding of the Prince and Princess of Wales in 1981. When the Marchioness died in 1988 he was the only non-family member to attend the private interment at the Royal Burial Ground, Frogmore, Windsor.

PREFACE

The extended Royal Family of the 20th century owes its origin to Queen Victoria who declared that the children of her daughters, Princess Helena (Princess Christian of Schleswig-Holstein) and Princess Beatrice (Princess Henry of Battenberg); those of her granddaughter, Victoria, Princess Louis of Battenberg and the children and grandchildren of her cousin, Princess Mary Adelaide, Duchess of Teck, would be members of the "Official" Royal Family. They were, of course, all members of foreign royal families, particularly the issue of Princess Louis who herself was born a Princess of Hesse. Their status within the family remained unchanged in 1917, despite the declaration by King George V that all those of his family holding foreign styles and titles were to adopt British ones. There emerged from this, two branches of Mountbatten (Battenberg): namely, Carisbrooke and Milford Haven. The Tecks became Cambridge and Athlone; while the two daughters of Princess Helena simply dropped the territorial designation Schleswig-Holstein, becoming princesses of "nowhere".

The direct heirs of the Princes who in 1917 received peerages used the courtesy titles of those peerages until they succeeded to the main title. In their fathers' lifetime, the second Marquess of Cambridge used the courtesy title Earl of Eltham, and the second Marquess of Milford Haven was known as the Earl of Medina.

It is the Sovereign's pleasure to determine who shall be designated a member of the Royal Family; who is "in" and who is not. During the present reign, there have been three occasions when the monarch has shown disapproval. The first wives of Lord Harewood and the Hon Gerald Lascelles appeared on the official list of "Precedence at Court"; their second wives never made the list. The name of Marina Ogilvy was discreetly dropped from the list following her marriage to Paul Mowatt in 1990. When Mrs. Wallis Simpson became Duchess of Windsor upon her marriage in 1937, she was famously excluded from becoming a member of the Royal Family.

Whilst there is no numerical restriction, it would seem that from the time of George V the "Junior" members of the Royal Family, as distinct from the Princes and Princesses of the Blood Royal, have been limited to the children of princesses who have married British subjects and to the grandchildren of the younger sons of the Sovereign. At the year 2000, the wider Royal Family comprises some 22 individuals. They and their spouses include: the son of Princess Patricia of Connaught, Captain Alexander Ramsay of Mar (80); the Duke of Fife (71), son of Princess Maud of Fife; and a grandson of George V, the Earl of Harewood (77). The remainder consist of the great grandchildren in the male line of George V, and the children of The Princess Margaret, Countess of Snowdon and Anne, The Princess Royal.

The junior members of the Royal Family are not nowadays expected to carry out official engagements or take on patronages. This was not always so as many photographs will show. The lesser-known royals took an active role supporting charities and numerous good causes. They put in many hours of unpaid work which often went unrecognised by the public and they were always on parade at official and family occasions: The Birthday Parade, Garden Parties, State Visits, Ascot, The Derby and events too numerous to mention where they added a colourful, dignified and sometimes eccentric presence. I hope that these photographs capture the spirit of those days, and breathe some life into these now almost forgotten figures.

The 80th birthday of Queen Mary, May 26th 1947, at Buckingham Palace. From the 1930s Queen Mary held large family gatherings on her birthday. These were held at Buckingham Palace and then later Marlborough House. A full list of those attending was published in the Court Circular. For her 80th, which was obviously a special occasion, The King and Queen gave a family lunch and those who attended are pictured here. This picture is taken from Queen Mary's own album. Standing from left to right: Lieut. Philip Mountbatten (Prince Philip of Greece), Lady Mary Cambridge, the Duchess of Beaufort, the Marchioness of Cambridge, the Marquess of Cambridge, Countess Mountbatten of Burma, Countess Toerring (Princess Elisabeth of Greece), Earl Mountbatten of Burma, Adml. Hon Sir Alexander Ramsay, Lady Patricia Ramsay, Capt. Alexander Ramsay, Col. Henry Abel Smith, Princess Marie Louise, Lady May Abel Smith, Lady Pamela Mountbatten, Lady Helena Gibbs, Princess Andrew of Greece (Alice of Battenberg) and the Marquess of Carisbrooke. Seated: The Duchess of Kent, The Duchess of Gloucester, The Duke of Gloucester, Princess Elizabeth, King George VI, Queen Mary, Queen Elizabeth, the Earl of Athlone, Princess Margaret, Princess Alice, Countess of Athlone, Princess Helena Victoria and the Dowager Marchioness of Milford Haven. In front: Prince William of Gloucester, Prince Richard of Gloucester, Prince Michael of Kent and Princess Alexandra of Kent.

Almost the entire Royal Family witnessed the Victory Parade from the Victoria Memorial in 1919. They are seen here walking from Buckingham Palace. Queen Mary, Queen Alexandra and King George V lead a large gathering of relations. Amongst others immediately following are: Princess Mary, in white, the Princess Royal, Duchess of Fife, Princess Helena, in black, partly obscures Princess Louise, Duchess of Argyll, Princess Alice, Countess of Athlone in white, to her left Princess Marie Louise and Princess Maud of Fife, Princess Arthur of Connaught in black hat, Princess Beatrice in white stole (?). The Duchess of Albany, and far left Princess Helena Victoria next to Lady Patricia Ramsay. The women are followed by King Manoel of Portugal, The Duke of Connaught and Prince Albert. The American and Australian flags were suspended from the front of the palace for the occasion.

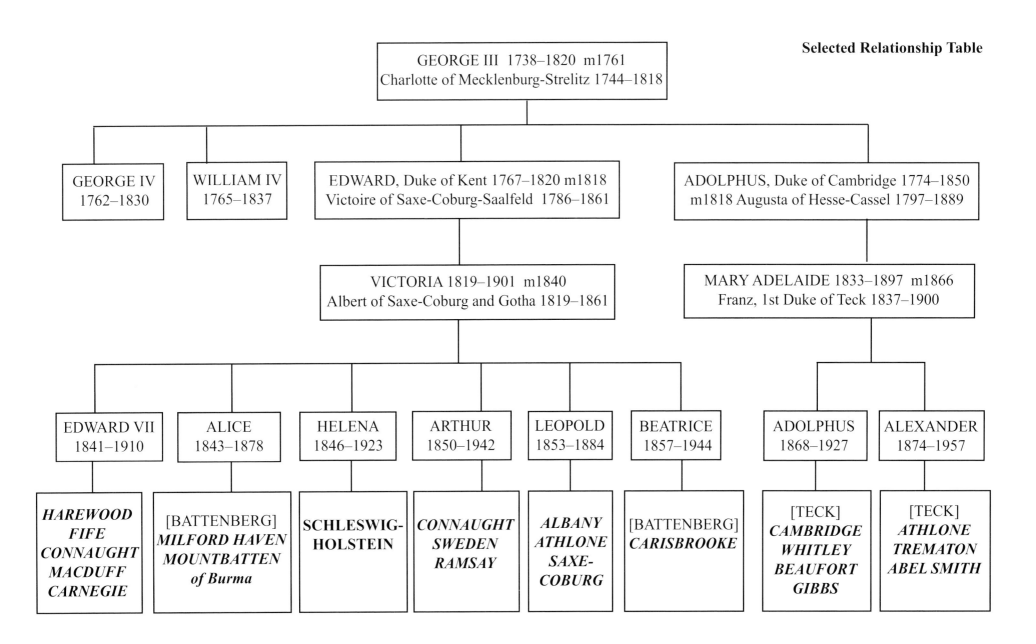

Selected Relationship Table

GEORGE III 1738–1820 m1761
Charlotte of Mecklenburg-Strelitz 1744–1818

- GEORGE IV 1762–1830
- WILLIAM IV 1765–1837
- EDWARD, Duke of Kent 1767–1820 m1818
  Victoire of Saxe-Coburg-Saalfeld 1786–1861
- ADOLPHUS, Duke of Cambridge 1774–1850
  m1818 Augusta of Hesse-Cassel 1797–1889

VICTORIA 1819–1901 m1840
Albert of Saxe-Coburg and Gotha 1819–1861

MARY ADELAIDE 1833–1897 m1866
Franz, 1st Duke of Teck 1837–1900

- EDWARD VII 1841–1910
  HAREWOOD FIFE CONNAUGHT MACDUFF CARNEGIE
- ALICE 1843–1878
  [BATTENBERG] *MILFORD HAVEN MOUNTBATTEN of Burma*
- HELENA 1846–1923
  SCHLESWIG-HOLSTEIN
- ARTHUR 1850–1942
  CONNAUGHT SWEDEN RAMSAY
- LEOPOLD 1853–1884
  ALBANY ATHLONE SAXE-COBURG
- BEATRICE 1857–1944
  [BATTENBERG] *CARISBROOKE*
- ADOLPHUS 1868–1927
  [TECK] *CAMBRIDGE WHITLEY BEAUFORT GIBBS*
- ALEXANDER 1874–1957
  [TECK] *ATHLONE TREMATON ABEL SMITH*

Trooping the Colour or, more correctly, The Birthday Parade, is the one occasion each year when most of The Royal Family appear on the Buckingham Palace balcony. Funerals and weddings apart, the Royal Family are rarely seen together. They are invited to the Trooping, not as one might imagine by the Queen, but by Queen Elizabeth The Queen Mother and are officially referred to as "Queen Elizabeth's guests". These two photographs date from the middle of the last century and show a varied collection of royal relatives.
1949 left to right: The Princess Royal, Prince William of Gloucester, The Queen, Princess Marie Louise, Prince Michael of Kent, Prince Richard and The Duchess of Gloucester, Queen Mary, The Duchess of Kent, Princess Margaret, the Marquess of Cambridge, Princess Alice, Countess of Athlone, Miss Elizabeth and the Lady May Abel Smith.

1951 left to right: Earl and Countess Mountbatten, the Marchioness of Carisbrooke, Lady Patricia Ramsay, Princess Marie Louise, Prince Richard of Gloucester, Queen Mary, The Queen with Prince Charles, The Duchess of Gloucester, King Haakon and Princess Astrid of Norway, Lady May Abel Smith, Princess Alice, Countess of Athlone and the Marquess of Carisbrooke.

A group taken outside Buckingham Palace following the wedding there of the Duke of Gloucester and Lady Alice Montagu Douglas Scott, November 1935. A full scale Westminster Abbey wedding had been planned. However, due to the recent death of the bride's father, it took place much more quietly in the Private Chapel at Buckingham Palace. Seen here, waiting to wave them off on their honeymoon, are from left to right: Lady Maud Carnegie, the Marquess of Cambridge, Princess Marie Louise, Lord Carnegie, Princess Helena Victoria, Princess Alice Countess of Athlone, Lady Mary Cambridge, Princess Elizabeth, Lady Patricia Ramsay, the Earl of Athlone and Mr Alexander Ramsay.

At the Coronation of Queen Elizabeth II in 1953, the Royal Box contained a large contingent of The Duke of Edinburgh's close relations. At the time of his wedding to Princess Elizabeth in 1947, it was considered too close to the end of the War to invite his three surviving sisters, as all were married to German princes. The day after the wedding The Duchess of Kent and Queen Frederica of Greece were dispatched to Germany to give a first-hand account to the slighted relatives. First row (l to r): Princess Alexandra of Kent, The Duchess of Kent, the Princess Royal, Queen Elizabeth The Queen Mother, Prince Charles, Princess Margaret, Prince William of Gloucester and The Duchess of Gloucester. Second row (l to r): Adml. Hon Sir Alexander and Lady Patricia Ramsay, Prince Michael of Kent, Princess Andrew of Greece, the Margrave and Margravine of Baden, the Prince and Princess of Hohenlohe-Langenburg and the Countess of Harewood. Third row (l to r): Lady May Abel Smith, the Marchioness and Marquess of Cambridge, the Marchioness of Carisbrooke, Princess Marie Louise, Capt. Alexander Ramsay, Prince and Princess Georg of Hanover and Earl Mountbatten of Burma.

The marriage in 1960 in Westminster Abbey of Princess Margaret and Anthony Armstrong-Jones was ignored by all European reigning houses, with the exception of Denmark, which was represented by her godmother, Queen Ingrid. The junior members of the Royal Family, however, turned up in force. It will be noticed that Earl Mountbatten is the only person wearing uniform. The bridegroom held no service rank and therefore morning coat was the order of the day. Such niceties, however, were not observed by Lord Mountbatten, who could not resist the opportunity to show off his many medals and decorations.
Back row, right to left: Hon Gerald and Mrs Lascelles, Lady Patricia and Adml. Hon Sir Alexander Ramsay, the Duke and Duchess of Fife, Capt. Alexander and Hon Mrs Ramsay and Earl Mountbatten. Middle row, right to left: The Duchess of Kent, the Duke of Kent, Princess Alexandra and Prince Michael of Kent, Princess Alice, Countess of Athlone, Princes Richard and William of Gloucester, the Countess and Earl of Harewood. Front row, right to left: The Queen, Prince Philip, Queen Elizabeth The Queen Mother, Prince Charles, Queen Ingrid of Denmark, The Duke and Duchess of Gloucester and the Princess Royal..

Princess Mary, with Viscount Lascelles holding George, their elder son, and their younger son, Gerald, lying in an elaborate cradle, 1924. Princess Mary had married the much older Viscount Lascelles in 1922 to the dismay of many members of the public who felt she was being sacrificed for a wealthy spouse. However, they got on very well having many shared interests and spending much time together in the country.

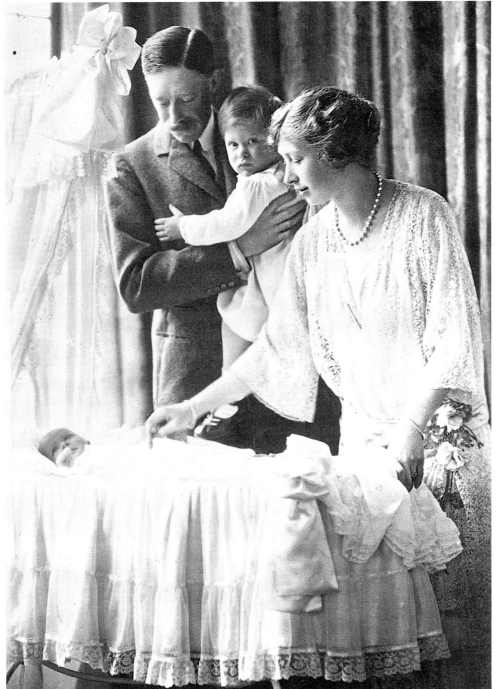

Princess Mary's sons, 1928. Their father had not yet succeeded to the Harewood title and so the boys were known as the Hon. George and the Hon. Gerald Lascelles. George became Viscount Lascelles in 1929 upon the death of his paternal grandfather. They are portrayed in patriotic mood.

The engagement of the Earl of Harewood and Miss Marion Stein 1949.
The Princess Royal is photographed with the engaged couple at Harewood House. Both Lord Harewood and his fiancé were professionally involved with the world of classical music; she being a concert pianist whilst he was involved with operatic productions. Their marriage ended in divorce in 1967. Lord Harewood in 1981 published an extremely erudite autobiography, entitled "The Tongs and the Bones" - a quotation from "A midsummer night's dream".

The Princess Royal with her grandsons at Harewood House.
Her grandchildren provided much pleasure to the Princess who was shy and somewhat stiff by nature. In their company, she relaxed completely, behaving as she once said, "as though I was a girl back at York Cottage". She is seen in 1958 with the children of her elder son, Lord Harewood, and their pet donkey. From the left: The Hon James Lascelles, the Hon Jeremy Lascelles and David, Viscount Lascelles.

The Hon Gerald Lascelles, younger son of Mary, Princess Royal, spent most of his life as an editor for jazz magazines and developing the Silverstone car-racing circuit. After his first marriage in 1952 he and his wife, the former Angela Dowding, moved to Fort Belvedere, a house forever linked with the Abdication Crisis. This photograph taken in the library there shows them with their only son, Henry. Gerald, in common with his brother Lord Harewood, incurred disapproval within court circles by having a child born out of wedlock whilst still both married to their first wives. As a result, both brothers were not invited to a number of family events. Lord Harewood was particularly saddened at not being asked to the funeral of his uncle The Duke of Windsor, to whom he was quite close. Gerald married secondly Elizabeth Collingwood, the mother of his younger son, Martin. After living outside Cirencester for many years, they moved to Southwest France, enjoying a happy life together until Gerald died at the age of seventy-four.

▶

The Hon. Gerald Lascelles and his second wife, 'Lisa', enjoyed a happy and carefree life at their French home where they created a garden in which some of his ashes now lie. This photograph taken by their son in August 1997 shows them relaxing at a village restaurant nearby.

15

Albany – Teck

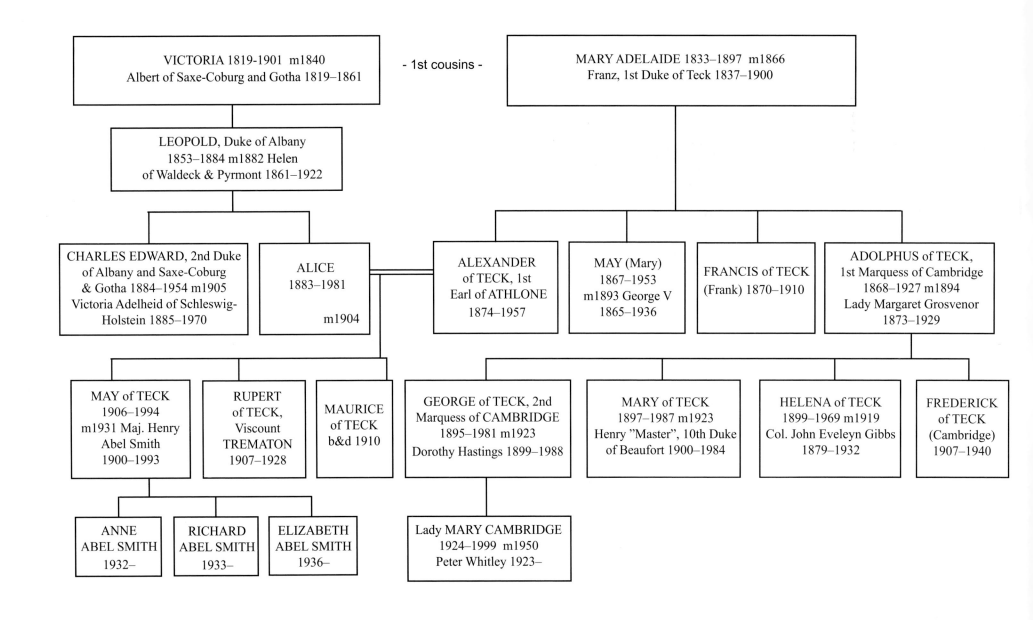

VICTORIA 1819-1901 m1840
Albert of Saxe-Coburg and Gotha 1819–1861

- 1st cousins -

MARY ADELAIDE 1833–1897 m1866
Franz, 1st Duke of Teck 1837–1900

LEOPOLD, Duke of Albany
1853–1884 m1882 Helen
of Waldeck & Pyrmont 1861–1922

CHARLES EDWARD, 2nd Duke
of Albany and Saxe-Coburg
& Gotha 1884–1954 m1905
Victoria Adelheid of Schleswig-
Holstein 1885–1970

ALICE
1883–1981

m1904

ALEXANDER
of TECK, 1st
Earl of ATHLONE
1874–1957

MAY (Mary)
1867–1953
m1893 George V
1865–1936

FRANCIS of TECK
(Frank) 1870–1910

ADOLPHUS of TECK,
1st Marquess of Cambridge
1868–1927 m1894
Lady Margaret Grosvenor
1873–1929

MAY of TECK
1906–1994
m1931 Maj. Henry
Abel Smith
1900–1993

RUPERT
of TECK,
Viscount
TREMATON
1907–1928

MAURICE
of TECK
b&d 1910

GEORGE of TECK, 2nd
Marquess of CAMBRIDGE
1895–1981 m1923
Dorothy Hastings 1899–1988

MARY of TECK
1897–1987 m1923
Henry "Master", 10th Duke
of Beaufort 1900–1984

HELENA of TECK
1899–1969 m1919
Col. John Eveleyn Gibbs
1879–1932

FREDERICK
of TECK
(Cambridge)
1907–1940

ANNE
ABEL SMITH
1932–

RICHARD
ABEL SMITH
1933–

ELIZABETH
ABEL SMITH
1936–

Lady MARY CAMBRIDGE
1924–1999 m1950
Peter Whitley 1923–

The Duchess of Albany with two of her grandsons, Prince Maurice of Teck and Prince Leopold of Saxe-Coburg and Gotha, in 1910. She is wearing mourning for her brother-in-law, King Edward VII, and later that year she was to mourn the loss of Maurice Teck. He died very suddenly whilst on holiday with his parents, visiting The Duke and Duchess of Saxe-Coburg at Schloss Reinhardsbrunn. His sister May recalled that one day he was crawling around, the next day he was not to be seen and all the adults were subdued. A few days later she was taken to his tiny grave and told that "Maurice has gone to the angels".

The Duchess of Albany like her mother-in-law, Queen Victoria, always wore a widow's cap indoors. A cheerful, fun-loving mother, she did not, however, approve of the cult of mourning as practised at the Court of Queen Victoria. A devout woman, she worshipped regularly at Esher Parish Church, where she preferred to sit in the front pew, rather than use the isolated Royal Gallery. This egalitarian practice once produced an embarrassing incident. Whilst at prayer, she thought that her hair had become loose. Discreetly placing her hands on her bun, she began re-pinning it, only to hear a muffled "Stop!" from the pew behind. To her horror, she found she had attached, to her own hair, the long white beard of an old man, kneeling behind her. A photograph taken at Claremont about 1912.

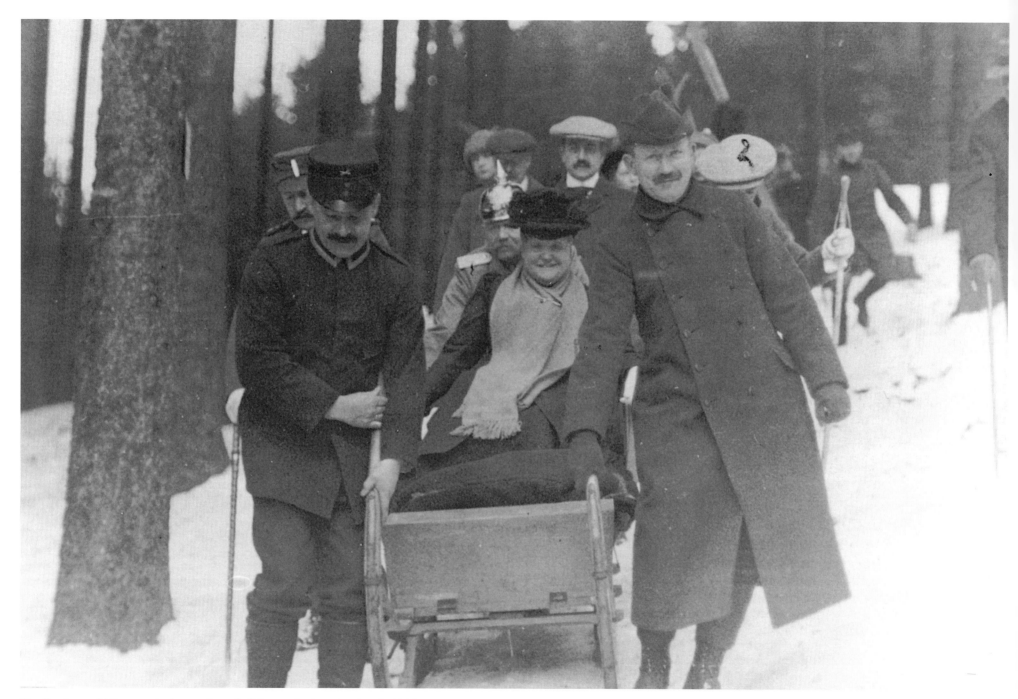

The Duchess of Albany enjoying a winter holiday in the Austrian Tyrol c1913. Her son's staff are bravely holding her toboggan at a steady pace in case it should slide away down the hillside.

Hinterris, Austria 1922.
The Duchess of Albany fondly holding the hand of her son,
Charles Edward, the Duke of Saxe-Coburg and Gotha. His wife,
Victoria Adelheid, who was always known as "Dick", is at the
right. This was taken during the last visit made by the Duchess
to her son.

The last photograph of the Duchess of Albany, taken with her son Charles Edward, Duke of Saxe-Coburg and Gotha, a few days
before her sudden death in 1922. She was staying with him and his family at their hunting lodge at Hinterris in the Austrian Tyrol
when she suffered a fatal heart attack. She had been so horrified with the protracted arrangements for her husband's funeral
following his death in Cannes and burial at Windsor that she left instructions to be buried where she died. Consequently, her
grave is on a hillside at Hinterris and a chapel was subsequently built nearby.

Princess Alice, Countess of Athlone, spending a holiday at Scheveningen, outside The Hague, in December 1923, with her aunt, Queen Emma of the Netherlands. Lady May Cambridge is also in the picture. None is suitably dressed for walking along the beach. After the death of her mother in 1922, Princess Alice became increasingly close to her aunt, visiting her at regular intervals.

For several years after the First World War it was not possible for Princess Alice, Countess of Athlone, to visit her brother the Duke of Saxe-Coburg and Gotha at his home in Germany. They used to meet in Holland at the palace of their aunt, Queen Emma. This group standing behind Queen Emma was taken c.1925 and shows Lady May Cambridge, Princess Alice, Viscount Trematon and the Duke of Saxe-Coburg and Gotha.

*Princess Alice, Countess of Athlone, believed in introducing her children to royal duties at an early age. She is seen here (centre) during the First World War with her daughter, May, and son, Rupert, visiting an Officers' Comfort Station. The other women are members of the Comforts Committee. At the time of her death in 1981, it was reported that she had carried out over 20,000 engagements as a member of the Royal Family. Although Queen Elizabeth The Queen Mother, has lived to be 100, Princess Alice, who died a few weeks before her 98th birthday, still holds the record of being the oldest member of the Royal Family by **birth**.*

A portrait c1914 shows Princess Alice with her two surviving children Rupert and May. May was educated at home, which was the Henry III Tower at Windsor Castle, where her father was Governor. It was from the roof of this tower that as a girl of four she watched the funeral procession of King Edward VII on its way to St George's Chapel. As the cortege wound slowly past, she remarked, incredulously to her nanny, "What, Uncle Bertie in a box!". A bright girl she later attended St. Paul's School for Girls at Hammersmith, travelling each day by omnibus from the Kensington Palace apartment of her grandmother, the Duchess of Albany.

A Picnic at Balmoral 1930.
The men went out early with the guns and were joined by the ladies for an al-fresco lunch. This photograph, taken by Princess Alice, shows Queen Mary with her brother, Lord Athlone, and King George V on the right. The Duke of York can be glimpsed to the left of Queen Mary.

Kensington Palace 1937.
Dressed for the Coronation of King George VI, Princess Alice and the Earl of Athlone with relations and household pose in the drawing room of Clock House. Seated: Princess Alice Countess of Athlone wearing the coronet and robes of a Princess of the Blood Royal, the Earl of Athlone with the robes and coronet of his rank and Lady May Abel Smith. Standing: Mrs. James Mure (Lady-in-Waiting), Lord Frederick Cambridge, Miss Janet Harkness (private secretary), Major Reggie Hargreaves (ADC), Baroness Imma Dornberg (cousin of Princess Alice) and Major Henry Abel Smith in the uniform of the Blues.

A sufferer from haemophilia, Viscount Trematon was the elder son of Prince Alexander of Teck and Princess Alice of Albany. Known as Prince Rupert of Teck until 1917, he had the dark good looks of his paternal grandfather, the first Duke of Teck, which Queen Victoria had greatly admired. His mother would never admit that there was anything really wrong with him, possibly as a result of having already lost a son from a cot death. In 1928 he went on a motoring holiday to France accompanied by some fellow Etonians. They were involved in a head-on collision. One night, while recovering in hospital, Rupert dreamt he was dying. His cries brought nurses rushing to his bedside. They tried to staunch the flow of blood brought on by his bandages becoming dislodged during his nightmarish struggle; alas to no avail. His cousin Lord Cambridge, who had previously visited him and was preparing to bring him home to convalesce, now found it was in fact his body he returned with and had to perform the sad task of informing Queen Mary that Rupert had died. He was just 19 in this photograph.

The Eton and Harrow Cricket Match was a highlight of the social season during the 1920s and 30s. The Earl of Athlone and Princess Alice, accompanied by their son, Rupert, an Eton pupil, at Lord's Cricket Ground, London 1923.

Government House, Ottawa 1942. As Governor General of Canada, Lord Athlone represented the Sovereign at the State Opening of Parliament. They are shown standing in front of the official painting of Queen Victoria which appears in most vice-regal establishments. Once when arriving at an official function in Toronto, an over-zealous aide pulled open the car door so fiercely that it fell off, leaving Lord Athlone to clamber over it in as dignified a manner as he could muster.

Princess Alice, Countess of Athlone, with Lord Athlone on her left and Lord Frederick Cambridge on her right in Saudi Arabia, 1938. Lord Frederick, a bachelor, acted as ADC to his uncle on overseas visits. They had previously been to India where in Bombay they had stayed in bungalows in the grounds of Government House. Freddie wrote to his sister, Ilona (Lady Helena Gibbs): "On our way to dinner at the big house, we proceeded in a pompous manner along a red carpet which stretched from our bungalows to the terrace. On the way back, a dog had left a large 'calling card' in the middle, which meant our procession had to divide in a somewhat hurried and undignified fashion".

The wedding of Lady May Cambridge and Major Henry Abel Smith 1931.
Lady May was the first Royal bride to omit the word "obey" at her marriage service, which took place in the village church at Balcombe, a few miles from Brantridge Park where her parents lived. It was here that her cousins, Prince Gustav Adolf of Sweden and Princess Sibylla of Saxe-Coburg and Gotha, met and fell in love, marrying later in Coburg. Back row from left to right: The Hon Imogen Rhys, Miss Kathleen Alington, Princess Ingrid of Sweden, Maj. Hon Cecil Weld-Forester (best man), bridegroom and bride, Princess Sibylla of Saxe-Coburg and Gotha, Miss Verena Seymour and Miss Phyllis Seymour-Holm. Front row: Miss Jennifer Bevan, Miss Wenefryde Tabor, Lady Mary Cambridge, Princess Elizabeth of York, Miss Rosemary Fraser and Lady Alice Montagu Douglas Scott (later Duchess of Gloucester).

The Earl of Athlone and Colonel Henry Abel Smith, 1947.
They are photographed by Princess Alice in the quadrangle of Buckingham Palace after The King's Birthday Parade. Lord Athlone held the office of Gold Stick-in-Waiting whilst Col. Abel Smith was Silver Stick-in-Waiting.

Lady May Cambridge at the time of her engagement to Major Henry Abel Smith in 1931. Her fiancé was an ADC to her father during his time as Governor General of South Africa. Her parents did not initially approve of the match; they felt she ought to meet other men first. There was also a wish on their part for a grander union, probably from the higher echelons of the aristocracy. They reckoned without their daughter's strong-minded persistence. The marriage eventually took place in October 1931 and was to last for over 61 years.

A group taken in 1932 at Kensington Palace before Anne Abel Smith was christened at St.Mary Abotts Church. From left to right: Major Henry Abel Smith, his sister Helen, the nanny holding Anne, Lady May Abel Smith, the Earl of Athlone and Princess Alice. The nanny or, more correctly, the monthly nurse, was brought out of retirement for these occasions. She appeared in the same role at the christenings of Richard and Elizabeth Abel Smith. Anne is wearing the Christening Robe, which had been first used for Queen Mary and her three brothers.

Government House, Ottawa, 1940. This photograph was sent by Princess Alice, Countess of Athlone, to Major Henry Abel Smith, whilst he was on active service in the Second World War. She has written on the reverse, "we sat for a picture for a leading women's paper, and had great difficulty to keep serious, hence the very strained looks, except for Richard".
Left to right, Richard Abel Smith, Princess Alice, Anne Abel Smith, Lady May and Elizabeth Abel Smith.

A line-up at Brantridge Park, Balcombe, Sussex 1936. The Athlones regularly hosted weekend parties at their country home. This informal shot, taken outside the drawing room, shows them wearing mourning for King George V.
(l to r): Princess Alice, Lord Athlone, Countess Imma Dornberg (a cousin of Princess Alice, of Waldeck descent), the Duchess of Gloucester, the Duke and Duchess of Kent, and Lord Morven Cavendish-Bentinck a son of the Duke of Portland, who was invited by Princess Alice as a possible husband for Imma. Nothing came of her matchmaking, Lord Morven not being the marrying kind.

Princess Alice, Countess of Athlone, dressed for a Debutante Presentation at Buckingham Palace in the late 1930s. She is wearing the Royal Family Order of King George V and below that the Order of Victoria and Albert. This was in fact the large Class One badge, which had belonged to her mother, The Duchess of Albany. She herself had been given the smaller Class Two. After her death in 1981, Lady May Abel Smith had the crowns detached and the cameos are now worn as brooches.

In 1958 Sir Henry Abel Smith was appointed Governor of Queensland and, to mark the occasion, some official photographs were released. Lady May is seen here wearing a diamond and marquise pendant, which had been a wedding present from several members of the Royal Family. Also as a wedding present, Queen Mary had given her some of the famous Cambridge Emeralds which she had retrieved from the mistress of her late brother, Prince Frank.

When Anne Abel Smith married David Liddell-Grainger at St George's Chapel, Windsor in December 1957, almost the entire royal family attended. A reception was held in the Waterloo Chamber and the large wedding group was photographed in the Grand Reception Room. As the Queen had been a child bridesmaid for the first time at the wedding of Lady May Cambridge, it was thought that Princess Anne would carry out the same duties for the bride. This was not to be and Princess Anne had to wait until 1960 for her debut at the wedding of Lady Pamela Mountbatten. One of the largest royal groups of that period is shown here. Back row l to r: The Marquess of Carisbrooke, Lady Patricia Ramsay, Lord Carnegie, the Marchioness of Cambridge, Lady Helena Gibbs, the Duchess of Beaufort, Sir Henry Abel Smith, Prince William of Gloucester, the Hon Mrs Gerald Lascelles, Richard Abel Smith, the Hon Gerald Lascelles, Prince Michael of Kent, The Duchess of Gloucester, Princess Alexandra of Kent, Prince Richard of Gloucester and The Duchess of Kent. Middle row: The bride and bridegroom (fourth and fifth from left), and the best man, Julian Byng. Royal bridesmaids in this row are Crown Princess Beatrix of the Netherlands (far left), Princess Irene of the Netherlands (eighth from left), followed by the bride's cousin, Countess Victoria zu Castell-Rüdenhausen. Seated l to r: Sir Malcolm Barclay-Harvey (step-father of the groom), Princess Sibylla of Sweden, Lady May Abel Smith, Queen Juliana of the Netherlands, The Queen, Queen Elizabeth The Queen Mother, Princess Alice, Countess of Athlone, Lady Muriel Barclay-Harvey (groom's mother) and The Princess Royal. On the ground: Princess Christina of Sweden is at far left and Elizabeth Abel Smith at far right.

St. James' Palace 1960.

A group taken after the wedding of Capt. Richard Abel Smith and Miss Marcia Kendrew.

Marcia had been a model and readily adapted to life as a relation of the Royal Family; more recently she has been Sheriff of Nottingham. The bridegroom's father, Sir Henry Abel Smith, and the bride's father, Major General Douglas Kendrew, were both Governors of Australian States at the same time, Queensland and Western Australia, respectively.

Standing left to right: Two bridesmaids, Mr. Tim Kendrew (bride's brother), Major General Douglas Kendrew, Lady May Abel Smith, Prince William of Gloucester, bridegroom and bride, Sir Nicholas Nuttall (best man), Countess Victoria zu Castell-Rudenhausen, Mr. David Liddell-Grainger, Mrs. Douglas Kendrew (bride's mother), Sir Henry Abel Smith, Princess Alexandra of Kent, The Duke of Gloucester and a bridesmaid.

Seated: The Duchess of Saxe-Coburg and Gotha, The Duchess of Gloucester, Princess Alice, Countess of Athlone, The Queen, Queen Elizabeth The Queen Mother, The Princess Royal, The Duchess of Kent and Mrs. David Liddell-Grainger with her son, Ian. On ground: Bridal attendants and pages.

Elizabeth and Lady May Abel Smith at an official lunch at Lennon's Hotel, Brisbane in 1958. Whilst her mother threw herself into the hundreds of duties expected of the wife of a state governor, Elizabeth embarked on a series of journeys around Australia. She was so busy travelling that she was not able to return to London for the wedding of her brother in 1960.

▶

Elizabeth Abel Smith grew to be an attractive and head-strong young woman, eschewing society's conventions. Her marriage to Peter Wise took place at St Paul's Church, Knightsbridge in 1965. She is shown here with her father, Sir Henry Abel Smith, surrounded by a barrage of photographers' flashbulbs. This marriage ended in divorce nine years later and a daughter, Emma, did not survive infancy.

34

A consuming passion the Abel Smiths shared was the breeding of Arab horses. They ran a highly successful stud at Barton Lodge, their home for over 60 years, wich is situated on the edge of Windsor Great Park. A photograph taken outside the house in 1957.

Sir Henry Abel Smith at the State Opening of Parliament, Brisbane, Australia 1960.
He was the last British Governor of Queensland and was also the last to wear a white plumed hat. He and Lady May returned home in 1966 after eight successful years. Thousands of people lined the streets of Brisbane as they made their farewell drive to the airport, many running alongside the open car to grasp the couple's hands.

35

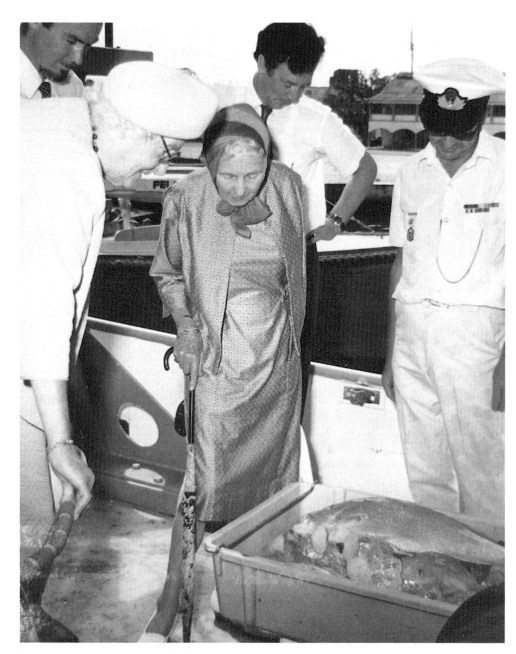
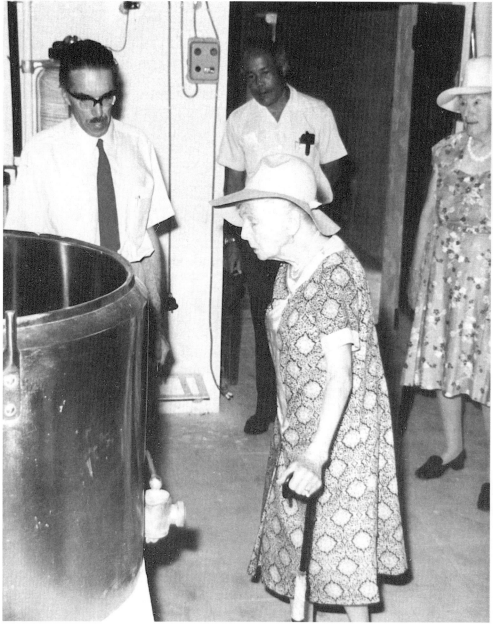

Princess Alice, Countess of Athlone, en route to, and in, Jamaica, in 1965. The Princess, along with her Lady-in-Waiting, Miss Joan Lascelles, would regularly travel incognito by banana boat, but on arrival in Jamaica, where she was Chancellor of the University of the West Indies, she became "Royal" once more, carrying out a full range of engagements. Two photographs from many in her private albums showing her waving the flag and being very much the Princess.

In her old age, Princess Alice became very friendly with King Gustav VI Adolf of Sweden, who is said to have proposed to her and was politely but firmly turned down. This did not prevent her from enjoying many Swedish holidays when she and the King walked and gardened. The left picture was taken on the terrace of the King's summer palace, Sofiero, in the south of Sweden in 1973. The king is pointing out a new azalea bed. Also visible is the Pekingese dog that belonged to the late Queen Louise. The right picture shows Princess Alice with King Gustav Adolf and Princess Sibylla, his daughter-in-law, who was also the niece of Princess Alice.

Princess Alice Countess of Athlone with her four great grandsons taken at Kensington Palace 1977. The boys are the children of Anne Abel Smith and David Liddell-Grainger. They are from left to right: Malcolm, Simon, Charles and Ian Liddell-Grainger. Princess Alice was 94 at the time and not long after fell, damaging her shoulder. She was taken to hospital but soon discharged herself; complaining that the nurses did not know how to apply her make-up!

Lady May Abel Smith on her eighty-eighth birthday, in 1994, taken by the author at Stonor, Oxfordshire. By this time she was starting to suffer from the effects of the cancer to which she succumbed in May 1994. This, however, did not prevent her enjoying a large birthday lunch followed by a vigorous walk along country lanes, talking non-stop and never pausing for breath.

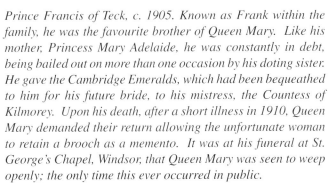

Prince Francis of Teck, c. 1905. Known as Frank within the family, he was the favourite brother of Queen Mary. Like his mother, Princess Mary Adelaide, he was constantly in debt, being bailed out on more than one occasion by his doting sister. He gave the Cambridge Emeralds, which had been bequeathed to him for his future bride, to his mistress, the Countess of Kilmorey. Upon his death, after a short illness in 1910, Queen Mary demanded their return allowing the unfortunate woman to retain a brooch as a memento. It was at his funeral at St. George's Chapel, Windsor, that Queen Mary was seen to weep openly; the only time this ever occurred in public.

Brothers-in-law, 1925. The 1st Marquess of Cambridge was President of the Richmond Royal Horse Show for many years. He regularly persuaded his sister, Queen Mary, to attend the opening day. He is shown here with his brother-in-law King George V walking the course.

Queen Mary was a regular visitor to the Shropshire home of her eldest brother Adolphus (Dolly) and his wife Margaret (Meg). She made constant forays into the surrounding countryside, scouring the village antique shops in the hope of getting a bargain or, better still, something for nothing! This photograph taken on the steps of Shotton Hall in 1926 shows (l to r): Lady Joan Verney (Lady-in-Waiting), Dorothy, Countess of Eltham, Dolly, Queen Mary, Meg and George, Earl of Eltham.

►

Margaret, Marchioness of Cambridge, photographed in the ensemble she wore at the wedding of her daughter, Mary, to the Marquess of Worcester (later Duke of Beaufort) at St. Margaret's Church, Westminster in 1923. She is wearing the sunburst brooch worn later by her daughter-in-law, Dorothy, at the Queen's Coronation. Around her neck are suspended the Rhedey earrings, which had belonged to the paternal grandmother of Queen Mary, Countess Claudine Rhedey, who was Hungarian by birth and had been killed as a young woman whilst watching a military parade. Her horse bolted into the path of the passing cavalry. Margaret, although fairly wealthy in her own right, was parsimonious, travelling third class by train. Once, in a crowded carriage going from Paddington to Shrewsbury for a ball, she wore a priceless tiara hidden beneath an old felt hat.

The eldest of three brothers, Prince Adolphus, second Duke of Teck and later first Marquess of Cambridge, unlike his son, George, was able to enjoy a successful life in the army, as befitted a nephew of the Victorian Commander-in-Chief, the second Duke of Cambridge. He spent many years as military attaché in Vienna where he was taken under the wing of Emperor Franz Joseph, spending much time at his court. He is shown here in 1914 in Bohemia.

Prince George of Teck taken at Cambridge Cottage, Kew, 1904.

Prince George and Princess Mary of Teck with their dog, Tim, 1900.
Always close, Prince George keenly felt the separation when his siblings went to live in Vienna during the time his father was Military Attache. His devoted mother felt the separation enormously sending him a postcard on an almost daily basis. In extreme old age he still had the collection intact and, although he himself was unable to see, his wife, Dorothy, would often read some of the more touching messages. This would sometimes bring on floods of tears.

The second Marquess of Cambridge would have dearly loved a full-time military career; unfortunately a chronic eye problem made this impossible. He was, however, an ADC Personal Staff with the Reserve Regiment of 1st Life Guards towards the end of the First World War. In later life he compensated for his unfulfilled military ambitions by amassing an enormous collection of prints, books, paintings and medals which his widow presented to the National Army Museum in 1981. He is pictured here at the time of the Silver Jubilee of his uncle and godfather, King George V in 1935.

The quiet wedding of the second Lord Cambridge (then known as Earl of Eltham) and Dorothy Hastings (pictured) took place at St Mary in the Elms, Woodhouse, Leicestershire in 1923. Her father, although of Plantaganet decscent , was not wealthy and therefore a large London wedding was out of the question. Her paternal aunt, Lady Kathleen Curzon,- Herrick had a house in Leicestershire and offered it for the celebrations which were attended by the Athlones as the sole royal representatives. They had to curtail their honeymoon in order to be at Westminster Abbey for the marriage of the Duke of York and Lady Elizabeth Bowes-Lyon, sixteen days later.

The Princesses Helena and Mary of Teck, with Prince Frederick, c1910.
The three youngest children of the Duke and Duchess of Teck spent much time together in Vienna before the First World War. Their eldest brother, George, was at prep school in England and missed out on much of their camaraderie. This was more than made up for during the long school breaks, when they would spend an idyllic holiday at Chocen in Bohemia, where their parents had a hunting lodge. The Kaiser, the Emperor Franz Joseph of Austria and many reigning German princes were guests at the same time for shooting parties.

Lord Frederick Cambridge taken whilst at Eton c.1922.
He was born Prince Frederick of Teck in Vienna in 1907. His mother was attending a performance at the Vienna State Opera when he made a premature arrival. There was no time to get her to the British Embassy and so Freddie was born at the rear of the Royal Box. When he was twenty-one, it was realised that he was an Austrian citizen and steps had to be taken to naturalise him as a British Subject. He became a professional soldier serving with the Coldstream Guards where he spent several years in Palestine. Anxious to attend the Coronation of King George VI, he wrote from Jerusalem to his sister Mary asking that "when old Connaught* comes to tea, be sure to press him that the regiment is back home for May". In May 1940 he was killed whilst fighting close to the French-Belgian border and lies buried at Herrent, near Louvain, Belgium.
* The Duke of Connaught, third son of Queen Victoria.

To denote their descent from King George III and not from Queen Victoria (the exception being Lady May Abel Smith who was descended from both monarchs), the Cambridges were known as the Old Royal Family. They always turned out in force for the Birthday Parade, as this photograph of 1928 depicts. L to R: Lord Frederick Cambridge, the Marquess and Marchioness of Cambridge and Lady Helena Gibbs.

During the first World War, the 1st Lady Cambridge allowed her house to be used as a convalescent home. In this photograph she stands in the centre with her children Mary, to the left, Helena (Ilona), to the right, and Freddie, seated at her feet. She had little faith in conventional medicine and died at the early age of 56, having consulted a vet rather than a doctor. In 1929, she became the first member of the Royal Family to have a funeral service at the recently opened Frogmore Burial Ground.

The Duchess of Teck (later Marchioness of Cambridge) with her daughters during the First World War. She is seen here picnicking at army manoeuvres on Salisbury Plain in 1914. Princess Mary of Teck stands next to her mother with Princess Helena sitting on the ground, and the governess, Miss Otz, seated at the left.

Lady Helena Cambridge married at St. George's Chapel, Windsor in 1919, Col. John Evelyn Gibbs.
He was many years her senior but they enjoyed a fulfilling marriage, living in the Gloucestershire countryside where they formed part of a large circle of hunting friends. In 1932 they had planned
to visit Jerusalem to stay with Helena's brother, Freddie. Just prior to leaving "Evie" Gibbs was stricken with a strange sleeping sickness from which he never recovered, dying after a few days.
Lady Helena lived on until 1969, when she died at Badminton, where she had been living with her sister, since suffering a stroke a year earlier. The bridegroom, bride and best man, Col. Lancelot
Gibbs (on the bride's left), are accompanied by a large retinue of attendants. Lady May Cambridge is the only Royal bridesmaid seen standing third from right.

The Duchess of Beaufort posing in the North Hall at Badminton in 1958. An active supporter of many charities, she frequently allowed Badminton to be used for all manner of good causes. She is about to attend a ball in honour of the R.S.P.C.A. Though small of stature; and, in fact, often mistaken for a guide when the house was open to the public, she could, when necessary, dress as a "grand dame".

On days when the house was open, she would sometimes be asked by a visitor if the duchess was around; "Oh, she's not far away" was her usual vague reply.

48

The Cambridge family had a long association with the Royal Home for Officers' Families, which dated back to early Victorian times. The first Duke of Cambridge had been its first patron, its last being the second Marchioness of Cambridge. She is seen in this photograph, right, with the newly married Duchess of Gloucester, who was paying her first visit to the home in 1936. Queen Mary paid a visit to the home in 1933. After being received by Lady Cambridge she was presented with a posy by the chairman's daughter; The poor girl made such an exaggerated courtesy that she toppled over in the process, her flowers landing under the table.

From the age of 10 the Duke of Beaufort was known as "Master", having then been given his own pack of hounds. In this photograph he and the Duchess pose outside Worcester Lodge, Badminton, wearing the distinctive blue and yellow coats of the Beaufort Hunt. She was riding side saddle into her late 70s. Despite her loss of short term memory in later years, she could still recall the events of her youth with great clarity. At 89, she sang faultlessly in German every word of 'Acht Nachtingall'.

The Duchess of Beaufort was hostess to her aunt, Queen Mary, at Badminton for the duration of the War. The Queen and a large entourage took up so much space that the Beauforts were reduced to living in a few rooms. Once when asked which part of the house Queen Mary had occupied, the Duchess wearily replied; "She lived in all of it". Queen Mary is seen with the Duchess on her left and the Duchess of Kent on her right at a tea hosted by soldiers billeted nearby.

Lady Mary Cambridge, with her great-aunt and godmother, Queen Mary, taken outside the kitchen door of Dallicot House, Bridgnorth, Shropshire, c 1927. Her parents bought this rather run down house quite cheaply. Queen Mary came to inspect and was shocked by the lack of grand furniture. She sent surplus items from the Royal Collection, which were returned, little by little, as they became more affluent and inherited family heirlooms.

The Marchioness of Cambridge pictured at an air show with the Prince of Wales c.1928. She was a competent pilot, often flying his aeroplane. Once, flying to Newmarket races, she circled the course looking for a nearby landing place. Upon arrival at the Jockey Club, she was asked to join King George V for lunch. All went well until pudding arrived, when the King fixed her with a beady eye: "And how did you get here today, Dorothy?", the King barked. "Actually, in David's aeroplane, Sir". "I knew that was my son's damn machine", he exploded. "I don't approve of aircraft near horses, and I don't like women flying!"

In Coronation finery, 1953, Lady Mary and Mr. Peter Whitley are photographed at their apartment in Hurlingham Court, West London, accompanied by the King Charles Spaniels from whom she was rarely separated. After her marriage, Lady Mary continued to attend royal events, but, as time went on, her appearances became less frequent though she never gave up Royal Ascot, where she was seen in the Royal Box on all four days.

Lady Mary Cambridge, the only child of the second Marquess and Marchioness of Cambridge, had been a bridesmaid at several royal weddings, the last being that of the present Queen in 1947. Her marriage in 1950 to Peter Whitley was not universally approved of. Queen Mary had wanted her to marry King Michael of Rumania, who was also a guest at the Queen's wedding. Lady Mary had ideas of her own and her marriage was a long and happy one. Because the bridegroom's parents were divorced, neither Queen Mary nor any of the major royals attended the wedding, the Athlones being sent to represent them. Lady Mary and Peter Whitley are seen leaving All Saint's Church in the village of Kirtling, near Newmarket.

Lady Mary Whitley with her children, Sarah and Charles, 1970. By now she had become a figure on the fringes of Royal family life. However, when her children were young they would be invited to the Queen's Birthday Parade, appearing on the Buckingham Palace balcony to watch the ceremonial fly past. Her final years were spent in Somerset where she created a most unusual garden from a virtual wilderness. She was never idle, moving around at great speed, doing several things simultaneously. During the war, as a teenager, she trained as a nurse at Poplar Hospital in East London. A much blitzed and damaged area, she chose to live and work there rather than at a safe hospital for officers elsewhere. As a girl she was very close to the present Queen. They were bridesmaids together, learned to ride and dance together and, as she once remarked, "we even caught flu at the same time". In spite of doubts expressed by some people back in 1950, her marriage proved to be a most perfect union and shortly after she died in 1999 a cousin remarked, "I am so glad that the disapproving were proved wrong".

One of the last royal occasions attended by the Marchioness of Cambridge was the wedding in July 1981 of the Prince and Princess of Wales. She had at first declined the invitation, feeling that, as she had attended almost every royal wedding since Princess Mary's in 1922, "enough was enough". Her plan was to install a giant television set in the village hall, where everyone was to be invited, and she herself would give a commentary. Due to the continuing frail health of her sister-in-law, Mary, the Duke of Beaufort persuaded her to accompany him to the service. This picture was taken by the author at St. James's Palace prior to leaving in a motor-car procession for St Paul's Cathedral.

Lady Mary Whitley brought up her children to be natural and un-affected. They lived outside Hurstpierpoint in Sussex, where these photographs were taken at the wedding of her daughter Sarah in 1982. The picture on the right shows Lady Cambridge with her daughter, Lady Mary. The picture on the left shows Sarah, her brother Charles Whitley and their mother.

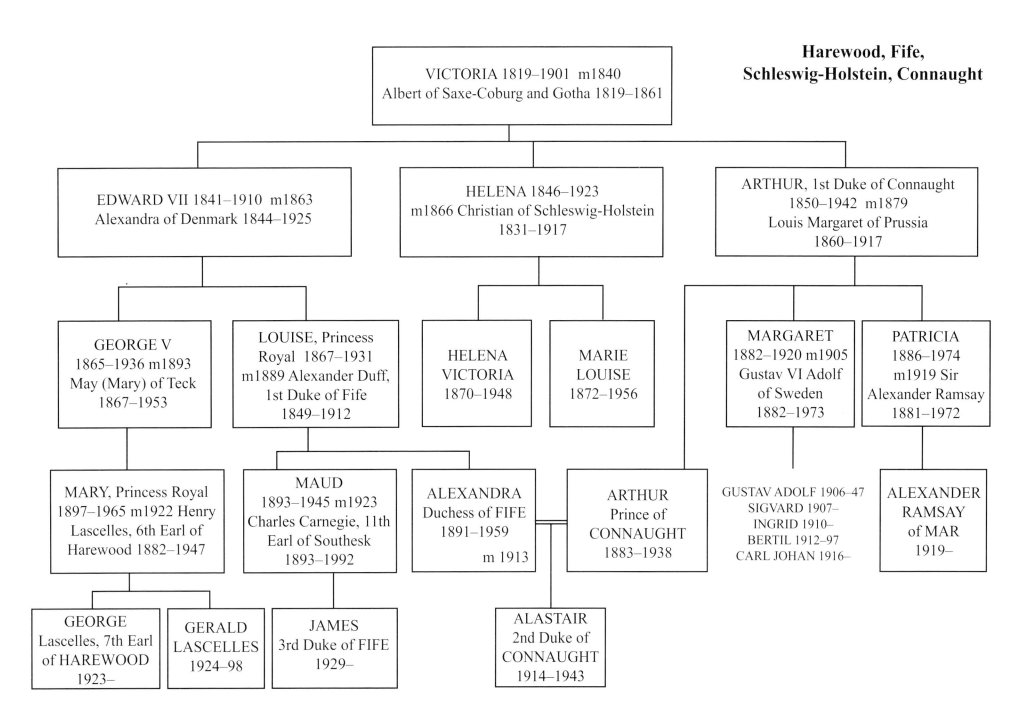

Harewood, Fife, Schleswig-Holstein, Connaught

VICTORIA 1819–1901 m1840
Albert of Saxe-Coburg and Gotha 1819–1861

EDWARD VII 1841–1910 m1863
Alexandra of Denmark 1844–1925

HELENA 1846–1923
m1866 Christian of Schleswig-Holstein
1831–1917

ARTHUR, 1st Duke of Connaught
1850–1942 m1879
Louis Margaret of Prussia
1860–1917

GEORGE V
1865–1936 m1893
May (Mary) of Teck
1867–1953

LOUISE, Princess
Royal 1867–1931
m1889 Alexander Duff,
1st Duke of Fife
1849–1912

HELENA
VICTORIA
1870–1948

MARIE
LOUISE
1872–1956

MARGARET
1882–1920 m1905
Gustav VI Adolf
of Sweden
1882–1973

PATRICIA
1886–1974
m1919 Sir
Alexander Ramsay
1881–1972

MARY, Princess Royal
1897–1965 m1922 Henry
Lascelles, 6th Earl of
Harewood 1882–1947

MAUD
1893–1945 m1923
Charles Carnegie, 11th
Earl of Southesk
1893–1992

ALEXANDRA
Duchess of FIFE
1891–1959

m 1913

ARTHUR
Prince of
CONNAUGHT
1883–1938

GUSTAV ADOLF 1906–47
SIGVARD 1907–
INGRID 1910–
BERTIL 1912–97
CARL JOHAN 1916–

ALEXANDER
RAMSAY
of MAR
1919–

GEORGE
Lascelles, 7th Earl
of HAREWOOD
1923–

GERALD
LASCELLES
1924–98

JAMES
3rd Duke of FIFE
1929–

ALASTAIR
2nd Duke of
CONNAUGHT
1914–1943

Princess Helena Victoria photographed in 1939 and her sister, Princess Marie Louise, in 1934. These two were inseparable spending most of their adult lives under the same roof. Whilst they had a large circle of different friends they always appeared together at the same gatherings and became known within the family as "the orphans". Princess Helena Victoria was thwarted in love, consequently throwing herself into a lifetime of charitable works, notably her Presidency of the Y.W.C.A. Princess Marie Louise was altogether a more sanguine personality, who mixed freely with people of all backgrounds; she listed painters, costermongers, ex jail-birds, mediums, as well as many aristocrats, amongst her friends. She was also a tireless worker on behalf of many charities. Not long before she died, in less politically correct days, whilst making a public speech, she announced: "When I'm gone I don't know who will carry on with this sort of thing: I work like a black". When Princess Helena Victoria was alive she tried to rein in some of her sister's excesses: she was not always successful! Princess Marie-Louise was married in 1891 to Prince Aribert of Anhalt, who turned out to be homosexual - it is doubtful if the marriage was ever consummated. Upon her return to England in 1900, her uncle, the Prince of Wales, remarked in his Germanic intonation; "Poor Marie-Lou, she came back just as she vent..."

Princess Marie-Louise at a reception at the Italian Embassy in 1954.

Princess Marie Louise was not a Princess of Great Britain and therefore was not entitled to wear royal robes. Instead, she appeared in a long velvet train, portrayed here at the Coronation of Queen Elizabeth II in 1953. The princess, a great devotee of a strong gin and tonic, took her own ready-made supply into the Abbey at the Queen's Coronation. She partook rather too freely of this libation and, having had more in the Annexe after the service, had to be escorted quite firmly to her carriage by a young ADC. On the return journey to Buckingham Palace she insisted, in spite of the inclement weather, on having the carriage window open, where she half-hung out waving to the crowds. Each time the procession came to a temporary halt she lurched forward almost landing in the lap of the Earl of Athlone seated opposite her. Her cousin, Lady Patricia Ramsay, repeatedly asked her to close the window; a request which fell on deaf ears.

A prince with six princesses. This formal group was taken at St. James's Palace after the wedding of Prince and Princess Arthur of Connaught in 1913. Standing from left, Princess Mary, bridegroom, Princess Mary of Teck, Princess Maud of Fife and Princess Helena of Teck who is wearing the Coronation Medal of King George V. Princess May of Teck is seated next to the bride at what was the first of five occasions when she was a bridesmaid at a royal wedding.

The Earl of Macduff with his parents, Prince and Princess Arthur of Connaught, 1923. Although a regular soldier, King George VI did not think his cousin, Lord Macduff, suited to active warfare. In 1941, he was therefore sent to Canada to be ADC to Lord Athlone who was Governor General. Part of his duties involved preparing the "drinks tray", not exactly a suitable task for someone who had more than a passing interest in its contents. One freezing April night in 1943, after consuming a large quantity of whisky, he retired to his room, where he opened the double glazed windows. The following morning, he was found lying dead from hypothermia on the bedroom floor. He had succeeded his grandfather as 2nd Duke of Connaught in January 1942.

◄

The wedding of Prince Arthur of Connaught with his bride Princess Alexandra of Fife. She was also his first cousin once re-moved. This was the last royal wedding at which full court dress was worn and took place in 1913 at the Chapel Royal, St James's Palace. Although the bride was little-known amongst the general public, large crowds gathered to cheer the procession from the Chapel Royal to Portman Square, where the reception took place at the home of her mother, the Princess Royal.

An Anglo-Swedish union. In 1905 Princess Margaret of Connaught married at St. George's Chapel, Windsor Castle, Prince Gustav Adolf of Sweden, eldest son of the Crown Prince Gustav (V) and his wife Princess Victoria of Baden. The newlyweds became Crown Prince and Crown Princess in 1907 upon the death of King Oscar II. Princess Margaret was extremely popular in her adopted land, not least because she was warm hearted and unpretentious. Standing; Princess Ena of Battenberg (later Queen of Spain), Princess Beatrice of Edingburgh and Saxe-Coburg & Gotha, bridegroom and Princess Patricia of Connaught. In front; Princess Mary of Wales and the bride.

The lovely Crown Princess Margaret of Sweden, who was also very artistic and a truly modern mother teaching her children practical gardening and other useful chores.

Margaret and Gustav Adolf with their four elder children in 1915; Sigvard, Ingrid, Gustav Adolf and Bertil. A fifth child, Carl Johan, was born in 1916. Margaret´s early sudden death in 1920 left the entire Swedish nation in shock, as it did her English family.

After the early death of his daughter, Margaret, The Duke of Connaught took a close interest in his orphaned grandchildren. They often stayed with him at Bagshot Park or in London. This formal portrait of him and Princess Ingrid was taken around 1928.

Lady Patricia and Com. Hon Alexander Ramsay on their honeymoon, 1919. The marriage of the extremely popular Princess Patricia of Connaught was the first Royal wedding to take place in Westminster Abbey for 600 years thus starting the present day tradition. From being the nation's idol as a young woman she had become almost forgotten at the time of her death in 1974.

Lady Patricia and Admiral Ramsay with their son, Capt. Alexander Ramsay at the wedding of Miss Georgina Wernher and Col. Harold Phillips at St. Margaret's Church, Westminster, 1944. In her hat, Lady Patricia is wearing her badge as Colonel-in-Chief, Princess Patricia's Canadian Light Infantry. In the First World War, when resident in Canada during the governor-generalship of her father, this regiment was raised in her honour. She worked the Regimental Colours which were carried into battle throughout the War. Upon her death in 1974, she was succeeded by her namesake and god-daughter Patricia, now Countess Mountbatten of Burma, as Colonel-in-Chief. At the extreme right is Lady Ludlow, the bride's paternal grandmother.

The day before the Queen's Coronation a final rehearsal was held which was attended by the members of the Royal Family. Lady Patricia Ramsay is seen arriving with her son, who is carrying in a box what was meant to be his mother's coronet. This had been hurriedly collected from the bank vault and, in his haste, he had in fact got the coronet of his grandmother, the Duchess of Connaught.

Princess Arthur of Connaught selling game at a nursing fair in 1937. She was a fully trained nursing sister, having spent many years working in a variety of London hospitals. Not long after this photograph was taken, she opened her own nursing home in Marylebone. Crippling arthritis forced her to give this up in 1949; however, she boasted of having a Prime Minister, several actors and members of the Royal Family as patients. In her retirement, she wrote a detailed account of her professional life, entitled: "A Nurse's Story". Printed for private circulation, its author was named simply "Alexandra".

▶

Occasionally Lady Patricia Ramsay would be coaxed out of her private life to perform an individual royal engagement; though she never stopped attending family events. In 1960, she travelled to Menton, in the south of France, where she unveiled a memorial to her grandmother, Queen Victoria, who in later years spent holidays in and around Menton.

The Golden Wedding took place in 1969 of Lady Patricia and Admiral the Hon Sir Alexander Ramsay. By this time the couple were beginning to become infirm and both were quite deaf. They featured a couple of years earlier in a television documentary about old age: "Don't Count the Candles" by Lord Snowdon. They were filmed, hand in hand, walking around their garden, gently disagreeing with each other and shouting in order to overcome their deafness.

Lady Patricia Ramsay, photographed by the author, outside her home, Ribsden Holt, Windlesham, Surrey, June 1971. She had inherited the house from her aunt, Princess Louise, Duchess of Argyll, who felt sorry that she had no place of her own, almost always living with her father, The Duke of Connaught, either at Clarence House or Bagshot Park. Princess Louise had built the house with components made up from old buildings, as a retreat for herself. No member of her family knew she had this property. One day in 1915, whilst about to be driven through the gates onto the public road, the car of her nephew, King George V, drove by. Quickly crouching on the floor, she shrieked to her chauffeur, "The King! The King! back up the drive, quickly!"

The Princess Royal, Duchess of Fife, with her younger daughter, Princess Maud of Fife. She was born in 1893, as the Lady Maud Duff. In 1905 she and her elder sister were raised to the rank of Princess with the qualification "Highness" by their grandfather, Edward VII. The King was advised by Garter King of Arms that there was no precedent for such action; Edward VII merely replied "Do it". She lived a quiet, retiring life, spent mainly in the country until her marriage in 1923 to Charles Carnegie, later Earl of Southesk, when she then spent more time in London. Her character was somewhat amorphous and vague, not unlike her nephew, the Earl of Macduff: charming but feckless. An asthmatic, she died of a respiratory condition in 1945.

◄

The three Fife princesses.
From left; Princess Maud, Princess Royal (Louise) and Princess Alexandra.
They are all in deep mourning for the Duke of Fife, who had died not long before. Late in 1911 the entire family had set sail for Egypt when they were shipwrecked off the coast of North Africa. It took many hours to rescue them. As a result, the Duke developed pneumonia, dying after arriving at Aswan in January 1912. He was illegitimately descended from King William IV, by his mistress Mrs Dorothy Jordan. In his memoirs, Prince Christopher of Greece, an uncle of he Duke of Edinburgh, claims to have been secretly engaged to Princess Alexandra, her parents evidently putting a stop to it.

The wedding group of Princess Maud of Fife and Lord Carnegie (later Earl of Southesk) taken at St. James's Palace in 1923. Following her marriage at the Guard's Chapel, Wellington Baracks, Princess Maud ceased using her royal style and title, becoming Lady Maud Carnegie. Unlike Princess Patricia of Connaught there was no formal renunciation. It appears to have been a casual arrangement. It is said, that King George V when asked by a courtier what title she would use after her marriage, tersely replied; "Lady, it is what she was before". The King had not approved of his father's decision to upgrade the Fife girls to Princesses. In the back row the groom with his bride on his left and Lord Galloway, the best man. The bridesmaids are not royal.

The Earl of Southesk remarried in 1952 a widow, Mrs Ion Campbell. Because he remarried, he forfeited his status as a member of the royal family. He still attended family occasions, where he would be seated immediately after the royal family, though his name ceased to appear in the Court Circular. This photograph taken by Anne Abel Smith shows Lord Southesk with his son, lord Carnegie on his left and his wife on his right with her son from a previous marriage.

◄

The ninety-four year old Earl of Southesk, widower of Princess Maud of Fife, with his son the Duke of Fife, at the Guards Chapel, London, for the wedding of his grandson, the Earl of Macduff in 1987. Lord Southesk at this time was still driving around his Scottish estate shooting rabbits from the car window. He subsequently had a spell in hospital, and when his son went to collect him, he was shocked by the weight of his father's suitcase. It contained the old boy's dumbbells!

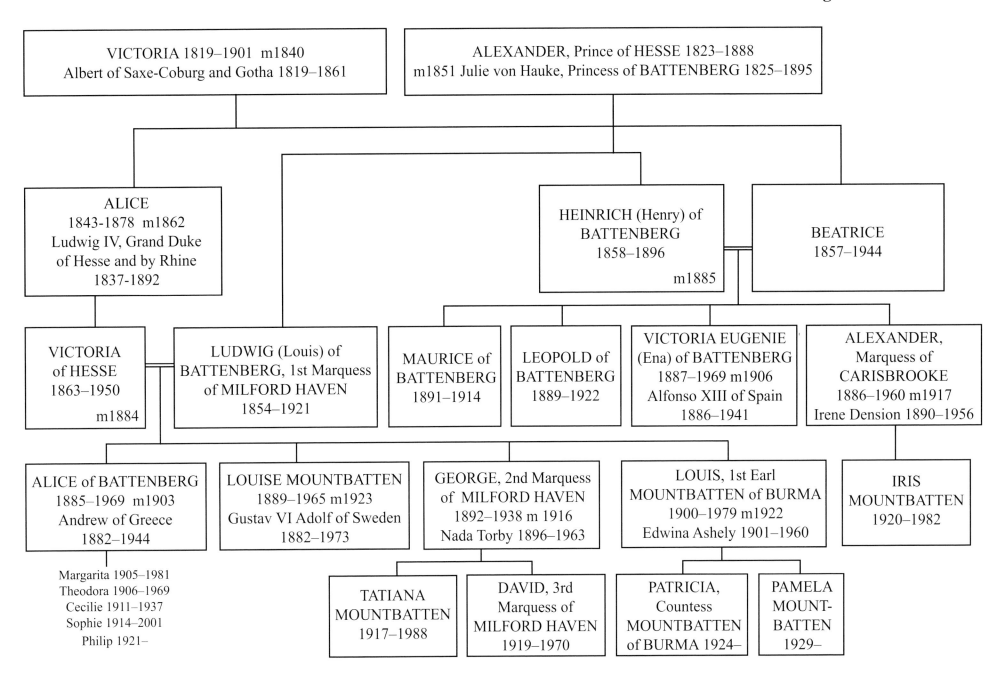

VICTORIA 1819–1901 m1840
Albert of Saxe-Coburg and Gotha 1819–1861

ALEXANDER, Prince of HESSE 1823–1888
m1851 Julie von Hauke, Princess of BATTENBERG 1825–1895

ALICE
1843-1878 m1862
Ludwig IV, Grand Duke
of Hesse and by Rhine
1837-1892

HEINRICH (Henry) of
BATTENBERG
1858–1896

m1885

BEATRICE
1857–1944

VICTORIA
of HESSE
1863–1950

m1884

LUDWIG (Louis) of
BATTENBERG, 1st Marquess
of MILFORD HAVEN
1854–1921

MAURICE of
BATTENBERG
1891–1914

LEOPOLD of
BATTENBERG
1889–1922

VICTORIA EUGENIE
(Ena) of BATTENBERG
1887–1969 m1906
Alfonso XIII of Spain
1886–1941

ALEXANDER,
Marquess of
CARISBROOKE
1886–1960 m1917
Irene Dension 1890–1956

ALICE of BATTENBERG
1885–1969 m1903
Andrew of Greece
1882–1944

Margarita 1905–1981
Theodora 1906–1969
Cecilie 1911–1937
Sophie 1914–2001
Philip 1921–

LOUISE MOUNTBATTEN
1889–1965 m1923
Gustav VI Adolf of Sweden
1882–1973

GEORGE, 2nd Marquess
of MILFORD HAVEN
1892–1938 m 1916
Nada Torby 1896–1963

LOUIS, 1st Earl
MOUNTBATTEN of BURMA
1900–1979 m1922
Edwina Ashely 1901–1960

IRIS
MOUNTBATTEN
1920–1982

TATIANA
MOUNTBATTEN
1917–1988

DAVID, 3rd
Marquess of
MILFORD HAVEN
1919–1970

PATRICIA,
Countess
MOUNTBATTEN
of BURMA 1924–

PAMELA
MOUNT-
BATTEN
1929–

◄

Princess Louis of Battenberg with her three younger children; from left: Prince Louis, Princess Louise and Prince George. Up to the start of the First World War, they led a peripatetic life, following her husband's naval postings as well as sojourns in England, Germany and regular visits to her sisters, The Empress of Russia and the Grand Duchess Elisabeth. Photo at Darmstadt c 1910.

►

Lord Louis Mountbatten with his bride Hon Edwina Ashley, Brook House, Park Lane, London in 1922. A glamorous couple, Edwina had the financial resources to sustain an enviable lifestyle. Her restless spirit found outlet in world travel and in leading a hectic social life. All this changed in 1939 when, following the onset of World War II, Edwina channelled her boundless energy into supporting the Red Cross and St. John's Ambulance Brigade. Completely fearless, she spent night after night giving support to the residents of the heavily bombed East End. Her work for the St. John's is legendary. She died suddenly in 1960 in North Borneo during a gruelling tour on their behalf. Standing; Princess Margarita of Greece, bridegroom, bride, The Prince of Wales (best man) and Princess Theodora of Greece. Sitting; Princess Sophie (third from left) and Princess Cecilie of Greece (far right).

The year before his death Lord and Lady Milford Haven paid a visit to their elder son and his family at Southsea. George, Earl of Medina, a naval officer based at Portsmouth, lived in a rented house. About this time, his wife Nada had been reported by a local doctor for driving fast and dangerously along Southsea Parade. When the case came to court, she sent a message via her solicitor to say that she had no intentions of appearing in front of a magistrate, as she was far too busy travelling abroad. This cut no ice; she was curtly informed that unless she appeared at a future hearing she would be spending some time as a guest of His Majesty!

On the left picture are seen seated; Victoria, Marchioness of Milford Haven, Georg, Earl of Medina with Lady Tatiana Mounbatten. Standing, Lord Milford Have and Nada, Countess of Medina holding her son David, Viscount Alderney. On the right picture are seen three generations of the male Milford Havens.

Lady Louise Mountbatten as a First World War nurse. She was a nurse in Bermondsey, South London, followed by a period in France. Before she became engaged in 1923 to Crown Prince Gustav Adolf of Sweden, the Swedish government was doubtful about her Royal status. A letter was sent to the Lord Chamberlain in London enquiring about her position within the Royal Family. A copy of the official precedence at court directory was sent to Stockholm. This clearly showed her name immediately after her brother Lord Louis and before the Marquess of Cambridge.

Crown Prince Gustav Adolf and Crown Princess Louise arriving at Kensington Palace for their wedding reception in 1923. The apartment of the bride's mother was too small for a large gathering and so Princess Beatrice came to the rescue, allowing her large central rooms to be used for the occasion. These had been occupied by Queen Victoria as a girl, and it was through this doorway that she left to take up residence at Buckingham Palace not long after she succeeded to the throne in 1837.

During his naval service Prince George of Battenberg, later Marquess of Milford Haven, travelled around the world. He is seen here wearing tropical uniform photographed in Honolulu, c.1912.

Nada, wife of George, second Lord Milford Haven, was a daughter of Grand Duke Michael Mikhailovitch of Russia by his morganatic wife Countess Torby. A somewhat exotic creature she was viewed with suspicion by some of the more staid members of her husband's family who felt she was too outre, with her Sapphic leanings. An adventurous traveller, she and her sister-in-law, Lady Louis Mountbatten, made several trips to the more remote parts of the globe, often sleeping beneath the stars. Pictured here at a New Bond Street studio c 1925.

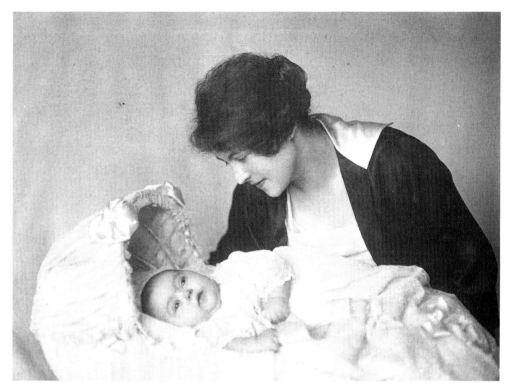

The Countess of Medina, with her daughter, Lady Tatiana Mountbatten, 1918.
When Tatiana was born in Edinburgh in 1917, her father, George, sent a telegram to his father,
the Marquess of Milford Haven, saying; "Tatiana has arrived". This caused great excitement
within the family since it was assumed that Grand Duchess Tatiana of Russia had escaped to
Scotland. No subsequent event in Tatiana's life caused such a flurry of interest.

Dressed for the 1937 Coronation wearing full dress naval uniform, the second Marquess of
Milford Haven had less than a year to live. He fell and broke his thigh in December. Cancer was
diagnosed and he died in April 1938 at The Empire Nursing Home in Vincent Square, London.
His cousin, Prince Arthur of Connaught was a patient there at the same time, suffering from
another form of cancer. In middle years he became somewhat of an inventor, being especially
interested in improving navigational equipment.

David, Earl of Medina, and Lady Tatiana Mountbatten, c 1925.
Even as a young boy, it was decided that he would continue the family tradition of joining the Royal Navy. He is shown here dressed as a rating from one of his father's ships. Tatiana, a sturdy girl with a streak of obstinacy, would often want her own way. Miffed at not being a bridesmaid at the Queen's wedding in 1947, she behaved badly at Buckingham Palace, where she had gone for the wedding breakfast. Deciding she preferred the seat which had been allocated to the King, she refused to move until Queen Mary threatened her with an umbrella.

George and Nada Milford Haven much preferred the warmer climes of the South of France to the colder Northern European holiday venues. They are seen above with their children, David and Tatiana, on the promenade at Cannes in 1933. An unusual photograph of the Milford Havens wandering along the beach at Deauville on their way for a swim.

Nada, Marchioness of Milford Haven, photographed on one of her last visits to England 1951. In 1948 she returned to live permanently at Cannes where she had been brought up. Increasing ill health made journeys difficult and she missed many major royal occasions, not least the Coronation of The Queen in 1953 and the funeral of King George VI in 1952. Her sister Zia, noticing that her name was not listed in the Court Circular as having attended the funeral, wrote her a sharp letter criticising her absence. She received a rather unapologetic reply, saying that she was definitely there; that in fact she had been in the second carriage and could not help it if this were incorrectly reported. She ought to have realised that she would not have been conveyed in such a prominent position, especially as the second carriage was filled with Members of the Royal Family of a far higher status than she enjoyed.

After the death of her mother in 1963 Lady Tatiana Mountbatten returned from France to live permanently in England. She had suffered from mental problems since birth which became more unmanageable as middle years advanced. For her last eighteen years, she was resident at St. Andrew's Hospital, Northampton, where she seemed happy and calm. She visited her relations frequently, being especially close to her nephews, George and Ivar (Marquess of Milford Haven and Lord Ivar Mountbatten) with whom she is here shown.

Coronations spawn a wide range of public events, many of which are attended by the wider Royal Family. A Naval Review takes place off Spithead, with the sovereign and royal guests on board the Royal Yacht. This snapshot taken in 1937 by Nada Milford Haven shows from the left: Lady Patricia Ramsay, Lord Milford Haven, Lord Louis Mountbatten, Princess Marie Louise, The Duke of Kent and Princess Helena Victoria.

At Coronations, some junior members of the Royal Family act as pages to their more senior relations. Here, the Earl of Medina was page to The Duke of Kent and carried his coronet in the procession into Westminster Abbey. In this group taken at Buckingham Palace in 1937, Viscount Lascelles, his brother Gerald and Alexander Ramsey were also pages at the same coronation. The Duchess of Kent is wearing a Russian fringe tiara.

The first Lord Milford Haven died suddenly in 1921 at the Naval and Military Club's residential wing in Half Moon Street, Piccadilly, following a short illness. In fact, his wife and daughter had gone out briefly to collect a prescription and, upon their return, found he had died. His widow, in deepest mourning, is at the centre of her family in this group taken at Netley Abbey. Standing (l to r): George, Marquess of Milford Haven, Princesses Margarita and Theodora of Greece and Lord Louis Mountbatten. Seated: Hon Edwina Ashley, later to marry Lord Louis, Nada, Marchioness of Milford Haven, Princess Andrew of Greece with Prince Philip and Lady Louise Mountbatten. Foreground: Princess Sophie of Greece, Lady Tatiana Mountbatten, David, Earl of Medina and Princess Cecilie of Greece.

◀

The Dowager Marchioness of Milford Haven is shown here at the door of her Kensington Palace apartment leaving for the wedding of her younger daughter Lady Louise Mountbatten with Prince Gustav Adolf of Sweden, 1923. She is accompanied by her elder daughter Princess Alice of Greece (at left), Prince Andrew of Greece and the Princesses Margarita and Theodora of Greece.

Not only did the Royal Dukes attend the State Opening of Parliament, but visiting relations were sometimes invited to attend, where they would be seated in the Royal Gallery. Gathered outside the entrance to the House of Lords in the mid 1920s are seen, from left to right: *The Marchioness of Milford Haven, the Countess of Airlie (the mother of Sir Angus Ogilvy), Lady Zia Wernher, Princess Margarita of Greece, the Marquess of Milford Haven, Princess Theodora of Greece (?).*

A sitting "Conga", taken at Lynden Manor in 1944. From left to right: Countess Zoya Poplewska-Koziel, Miss Myra Wernher (almost hidden), Nada Marchioness of Milford Haven, Miss Georgina Wernher, The Marquess of Milford Haven, Prince Philip of Greece, The Duchess of Kent, Sir Harold Wernher, Lady Bridget Elliot and Miss Parker (the companion to Lady Tatiana Mountbatten). Lynden Manor was the home of George and Nada Milford Haven and is where Prince Philip spent many of his school holidays.

Royal mourners and two brothers-in-law follow the coffin of Lord Milford Haven.
Right to left; The Duke of Kent, King George VI, the Marquess of Carisbrooke, Sir Harold Wernher and Prince Louis of Hesse and the Rhine. They are followed by foreign envoys.

The funeral procession in 1938 of George, Marquess of Milford Haven, en route from Bray Church near Maidenhead to the Bray Burial Ground, a mile distant. Full naval honours were provided and following the gun carriage can be seen his son, the new marquess, brother, Lord Louis Mountbatten, followed by King George VI, The Duke of Kent and the Marquess of Carisbrooke (in bearskin). The future Queen Louise of Sweden, Queen Victoria Eugenie of Spain and Princess Andrew of Greece were among the mourners. He and his wife lived nearby at Lynden Manor, where Prince Philip spent many of his school holidays. When Nada died in Cannes in 1963, her body was returned to Bray for a private funeral, attended by, amongst others, Prince Philip who was fond of his aunt, remembering her hospitality to him when young.

A group taken by the Crown Prince of Sweden at Sofiero c1935, which records a reunion between the Dowager Marchioness of Milford Haven (left) and her sister Princess Henry of Prussia (right). Lady Tatiana Mountbatten and the Crown Princess of Sweden complete the picture.

Rarely mentioning the subject, the Dowager Marchioness bitterly felt the murders, by the Bolsheviks, of her sisters, the Tsarina and Grand Duchess Elisabeth. The anti-German feeling at the end of the 1914-1918 war made it difficult for her to see her surviving sister, Princess Irene, the wife of Prince Henry of Prussia, a brother of the Kaiser. Eventually, through the good offices of her daughter, Crown Princess Louise, they were able to meet in Sweden.

The Dowager Marchioness of Milford Haven at Kensington Palace. c1947.
She had lived in the same apartment for almost thirty years, where she was constantly offering accommodation to members of her large family. Her grandsons, Prince Philip and David Milford Haven, both had attic rooms, and her daughter, the Crown Princess of Sweden, had a bedroom permanently at her disposal. The Dowager Marchioness was always preceded by clouds of smoke, a visible reminder of her dedication to nicotine inhalation. This, combined with her non-stop garrulous commentary, meant that her presence was all pervading. She had pronounced socialist leanings and did not enjoy formal court ceremonies. She was notably absent from the Coronation of King George VI. In 1917, George V, when reorganising the family styles and titles, wished her to be known as Princess Victoria, but she eschewed such pretensions, preferring to have the same status as her husband.

Princess Beatrice with her family, Osborne Cottage, Isle of Wight, 1910.
After the death of Queen Victoria, Princess Beatrice and her family moved into Osborne Cottage which was in the grounds of the main house. She regularly entertained her sisters and nieces and is shown here wearing mourning for the death of her brother, King Edward VII. Standing left to right: Princess Helena, Princess Patricia of Connaught, Prince Maurice of Battenberg, Princess Beatrice, a Miss Minnie Cochrane, Lady-in-Waiting to Princess Beatrice and Prince Alexander of Battenberg. Seated left to right: Prince Leopold of Battenberg, Queen Victoria Eugenie of Spain, King Alfonso XIII of Spain and Princess Helena Victoria of Schleswig-Holstein.

The eldest son of Princess Beatrice, Prince Alexander of Battenberg became Marquess of Carisbrooke in 1917 as part of the anglicising of the Royal Family. He served in all three services, first as a naval cadet and midshipman. This was followed by a period in the Grenadier Guards. This photograph, taken in 1915 and signed "Drino", shows him in the undress uniform of the Grenadiers. During the Second World War he spent time in the RAF where he was involved in "Intelligence". Having lived at the court of his grandmother, Queen Victoria, until he was 14, he had developed an inflated view of his position within the family. He married in 1917 Lady Irene Denison, the daughter of 2nd Earl of Londesborough.

Lord Leopold Mountbatten was the haemophiliac second son of Princess Beatrice. His early years spent with Queen Victoria had left him far less "affected" than his older brother. Outgoing and lively in spite of his physical handicap, he managed to persuade The King and Lord Kitchener to let him enlist in 1914. Serving as a Major in the KRRC, he was mentioned in despatches, and saw active service in France. A chronic hip problem made him quite lame and in 1922 whilst his mother was holidaying in Sicily, he was operated on at Kensington Palace and never recovered. This postcard of "Leo" was released for his 21st birthday in 1910.

Lady Iris Mountbatten with her mother, Lady Carisbrooke, 1920. She was the last born great-grandchild of Queen Victoria and was brought up at Kensington Palace, where her parents shared the apartment of her grandmother, Princess Beatrice. Her mother and father enjoyed entertaining theatrical personalities, who would often give impromptu performances after dinner. As a girl she was not allowed to stay up to watch the entertainment. This did not deter her and she would creep down the stairs, listening with fascination, by the half opened doors. When her grandmother died in 1944, she was told by her mother that, due to the separation from her husband, Major O'Malley, she would not be able to attend the funeral at Windsor. She then realised she had no future in England. She first travelled to India, ending up in America, where she held a variety of what were considered unsuitable jobs. She returned to England from time to time, the last occasion being for the funeral in 1979 of Earl Mountbatten, who was always kind to her. At the reception afterwards at Broadlands, apart from The Queen, few seemed to know who she was. She died in Toronto and was cremated there. Several years later, her cousin, Countess Mountbatten, brought her ashes to England, where they now rest in the Battenberg Chapel, Whippingham Church, Isle of Wight.

Taken outside Brantridge Park, Balcombe, Sussex, following the very quiet wedding in 1941 of Lady Iris Mountbatten and Captain Hamilton O'Malley. He was Roman Catholic and so Lady Iris relinquished her extremely remote place in the order of succession to the throne. The service had taken place at a Catholic Church at nearby Haywards Heath. The union was not a success and following a divorce in 1946, Lady Iris lived in America and then Canada, where she died in 1982. Two subsequent marriages were also failures, although a son was born in 1957 by her second husband Michael Bryan, a jazz guitarist. She was friendly with Duke Ellington who composed the song; "Iris Mountbatten, that satin doll". Lord and Lady Carisbrooke complete the group.

Lord Carisbrooke taken in 1956, just before the death of his wife. He was the first member of the Royal Family to enter the world of commerce, becoming a director of several companies. When he joined an Oxford Street drapery store as a director, he announced that he would spend one day each week serving on the shop floor. A dapper man, taken to wearing gold bracelets and rings, in later years he was described by the diarist James Lees-Milne as "reminding me of an old spruce hen cackling and scratching the dust in a chicken run - really, a typical old queen". When it was announced in 1919 that his wife was expecting a child, The Prince of Wales wrote to a friend: "I hear that Irene Carisbrooke is great with child and Drino has retired to bed for the duration". There was no love lost between the cousins, the Prince thinking him pompous and effeminate. His views on the Prince are not recorded.

The Marchioness of Carisbrooke 1949. Irene Carisbrooke missed becoming a Princess of Battenberg by only a matter of hours; her husband's change of title occurring the day before their marriage. This did not worry her in the least for she had a degree of the intellect shared by her cousins, Edith, Osbert and Sacheverell Sitwell, though she was a far less abrasive character. She suffered her husband's indiscretions with the male gender lightly, turning a blind eye and devoting her energies to many good causes. In 1931 she was staying in Madrid with the King and Queen of Spain, her brother-in-law and sister-in-law, at the time they were hurriedly forced to leave the country. She accompanied the Queen to the border, witnessing tearful scenes when Her Majesty took leave of her ladies-in-waiting.

From becoming a member of the Royal Family at her marriage in 1917, the Marchioness of Carisbrooke devoted her life to charitable works. She was a member of dozens of committees and frequently hosted charity balls and dinners. She is seen in this photograph with the Prime Minister, Clement Attlee, at a Mansion House dinner. ▶

The Marquess and Marchioness of Carisbrooke after the State Opening of Parliament 1939. They never missed this occasion, he particularly enjoyed the pageantry surrounding the opening and the opportunity to parade in parliamentary robes. After the event, she would regale her Sitwell cousins with stories of how some of the more ancient peeresses had appeared in dresses, which had seen far better days.

The Coronation of George VI, May 12th 1937.
An impressive gathering of British and foreign Royalty pose in the Throne Room of Buckingham Palace. From left to right; The Earl of Macduff, Lady Helena Gibbs, the Earl of Athlone, the Duchess of Beaufort, Princess Alice Countess of Athlone, Prince Bernhard and Princess Juliana of the Netherlands, Prince and Princess Arthur of Connaught, The Princess Royal and the Earl of Harewood, The Duchess of Gloucester, Queen Mary, The Duke of Gloucester, The King and Queen, The Duke and Duchess of Kent, Princess Eugenie of Greece, Queen Maud of Norway, Prince Frederick of Prussia, Crown Prince Olav and Crown Princess Martha of Norway, Lord Carnegie, Prince Nicholas of Greece, Lady Maud Carnegie, Prince Ernst August of Hanover, Crown Prince (King) Michael of Roumania, Crown Princess Ingrid and Crown Prince Frederick of Denmark, Prince Paul of Greece, The Prince Regent and Princess Paul of Yugoslavia and Lord Frederick Cambridge. Seated in front; The Hon Gerald Lascelles, Princess Margaret, Princess Elizabeth, and Viscount Lascelles. [Courtesy The National Portrait Gallery]

INDEX

Marlene A Eilers

QUEEN VICTORIA´S DESCENDANTS

1997, 2nd enlarged and updated edition.
192 pages, 168 illustrations.
ISBN 91-630-5964-9

SEK 295:- (c. £ 22 $ 34,50 € 32) + postage
[We accept major credit cards, VISA & Mastercard]

This is an encyclopedia of Europeean Royalty. Queen Victoria and her Albert had 9 children and 42 grandchildren. Of a total of 820 descendants around 450 are alive today, residing all over the world. Many of them are Kings and Queens, Princes and Princesses, Dukes and Barons. Many of them belong to various Royal Families, e.g. Spain, Sweden, Denmark, Norway, Russia, Prussia, Hanover and Hesse, but there are also ordinary people; workers, actors and secretaries.

This book presents them all; first in a fascinating text part where the lives and fates of the descendants and of the inlaws are vividly told; then in a second, genealogical part, where all details, full names, places, dates of births, marriages, divorces and deaths are shown in an easy-to-understand manner. 162 rare pictures, mainly focusing the lesser known royals, enhance this unique work. A detailed bibliography and index, holding several hundred different names completes the book.

COMPANION VOLUME

The corrections and updates covering the last 5 years, along with new interesting text and current photographs, are now available in a COMPANION VOLUME. 2003 80 pages, c. 80 ill.
SEK 150:- (c. £ 10 $ € 16) + postage

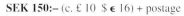

William Mead Lalor

ROYALTY BETWEEN THE WARS (1999)
ROYALTY AFTER THE WARS (2001)
ROYALTY BEFORE THE WARS (2003)

Each: 96 pages, c. 150 ill. large format [captions in English]

Three uniqe collections of European Royal pictures from 1900 to c. 1970, especially focusing the lesser known families. This is where you find the Schwarzburgs and the Wittelsbachs as well as the Bernadottes and the Windsors. Both formal and informal pictures and many Royal wedding groups with complete identifications. A treat for anyone interested in European Royalty. Order your copy directly from the Publisher.

SEK 260:– each

(c. £ 20 $ 32,50 € 30) + postage
[We accept major credit cards, VISA & Mastercard]

ROSVALL ROYAL BOOKS

Enåsen, 521 91 FALKÖPING, Sweden
TEL 46-515-37105 FAX 46-515-37165
e-mail ted.rosvall@telia.com
http://welcome.to/royalbooks

Send for our
FREE CATALOGUES
with over 500 Royal Titles
from 15 different countries.

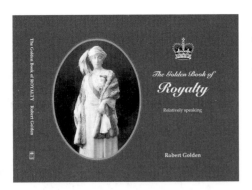

THE GOLDEN BOOK OF ROYALTY - Relatively speaking
by Robert Golden

Since 1827, the Court Circular - the formal list recording the official engagements carried out by members of the Royal Family - has been published in The Times and in the Daily Telegraph. During the reign of Queen Victoria it also recorded snippets of her private life, faithfully documenting the visits of her many descendants, both British and foreign. The Queen often drafted the wording herself in order to give prominence to events which she felt should enjoy a wide circulation. She would also use its columns to promote her own views, and phrases such as 'much pleasure' or 'great regret' frequently describe her reaction to events of the day.

Up until the death of King George V in 1936 the private comings and goings of the monarch's family were given equal importance alongside the official, often mundane, duties. It was with great regularity that one could read during the 1920s and '30s entries such as 'Princess Victoria, the Duke of Connaught, Lady Patricia Ramsay, Princess Helena Victoria, Princess Marie Louise and the Marquess and Marchioness of Cambridge visited Their Majesties today and remained to luncheon [or tea]'. The recording of these family gatherings gives one an insight into the closeness of the monarch and the extended family, providing invaluable material for historians and social chroniclers.

Many of the people who appear in the pages of this book have featured from time to time in the Court Circular. One would probably not be able to make such a claim when recording later periods of royal life. Unique pictures of the Connaughts, the Mount-battens, the Athlones, the Cambridges and the FitzGeorges as well as the Hesses, the Hohenlohe-Langenburgs, the Prussians and the Coburgs. Many "bejewelled and begowned" portraits as well as more informal ones. Informed and entertaining captions.

David McIntosch

DIE UNBEKANNTEN HABSBURGER
THE UNKNOWN HABSBURGS

A unique collection of pictures and pedigrees of the Tuscany (Toscana) branch of the Habsburg dynasty. Leopold Wölfling, the Crown Princess of Saxony and Johann Orth – they are all here.

HM KING MICHAEL I OF ROMANIA – A Tribute
SM Le Roi Michel Ier de Romanie – un Hommage

King Michael – his life in pictures, with text by his daughter and son-in-law. A unique life, a unique book! Dedications by the King of Spain and by the Prince of Wales. Pictures from the private albums of the Romanian Royal family.